I0162947

Been There Done That

Mike Miller

Father's House Press

Unless otherwise noted, all scripture taken from the New King James Version® Copyright © 1982 by Thomas Nelson, Inc. Used by permission. All rights reserved.

Been There, Done That ©2012 All Rights Reserved.

No part of this publication may be reproduced or transmitted in any form or by any means without written permission from the author or publisher.

For the *Been There, Done That* teaching series, book and other information, visit us - www.wordofgraceministry.com

Table of Contents:

Preface

There's a message from Jesus in John's Gospel that reveals the potential for each of us to live this life with a bold, invincible attitude regardless of the circumstances that confront us. This book will search the depths of His words and uncover the treasures hidden within them. In our discovery you'll be given ample opportunity to question and redefine the common interpretation of many of the scriptures we'll explore. I believe that if you'll open your heart to a fresh revelation of the grace of God you'll find a whole new confidence for fearless living in the days and years of your natural life.

Chapter 1

Let Not Your

Heart Be Troubled

John 14:1-3 — "Let not your heart be troubled; you believe in God, believe also in Me. In My Father's house are many mansions; if it were not so, I would have told you. I go to prepare a place for you. And if I go and prepare a place for you, I will come again and receive you to Myself; that where I am, there you may be also."

Heart attacks, heart failures, and a plethora of heart problems are major causes of death in the world today. Consequently we're bombarded with information about lowering our intake of cholesterol, eating a heart-friendly diet, exercising, watching our weight, etc. While that's all well and good, the words of Jesus above are God's answer regarding heart problems of every description, and His prescription for health. They were spoken by Jesus to provide us with confidence and peace through all of life's stressful happenings.

In the first sentence He proposes an end to all heart problems: "Let not your hearts be troubled; believe in God and believe in Me." That doesn't mean all our problems will go away with a wave of a magic wand. Jesus said in John 16:33 that we will always have tribulations in this world. However He wants to reveal a way that steers us through them without being shipwrecked and left stranded like a piece of battered debris on the beach of life.

Jesus tells us it's possible to arrive at a place where tribulation doesn't disturb our heart. If that is so then we won't have heart trouble in any form. The outer, physical person is a reflection of the inward state of our being - we learned that from 3 John 1:2: we prosper physically as our soul (mind, will, and emotions) prospers.

There are revelations in the bible regarding health that can affect different areas of healing if we allow them to become personal revelation. In this instance Jesus is focusing on heart issues. Let's visit another passage, Luke 21:26:

> Luke 21:26 "...men's hearts failing them from fear and the expectation of those things which are coming on the earth, "

The word for heart in the Greek, *cardio,* refers literally to the human blood-pump. Jesus connects fear, and dread of the future, to heart attacks. Interestingly, He didn't say hearts were failing due to high cholesterol, high triglycerides, high blood pressure, or too much bacon fat (not a problem for the Israelites!), or too much salt in the diet. Those things might exacerbate the problem but they aren't the root. The root of heart trouble is: fear, and the expectation of things to come.

Often the heart issues we deal with in later life began in our childhood, when we learned negative expectation from experiences or by example - in deed if not in word. We've often preconditioned body parts such as our heart-pump and arteries to be more susceptible to disease, by expecting the worst.

4

Jesus also did not attribute heart problems to the lack of Omega-3, CoQ-10 or any other known supplements. These may have a positive effect on the problem we've possibly helped create for ourselves, but Jesus was clear that our hearts fail us as a result of fear and the expectation (dread) of things to come (I take supplements and vitamins, I eat bacon at times, so I'm not condemning any of them). We, however, have been dealing with the effects of heart problems, not the cause. We've been dealing with the problems from the outside in, rather than the inside out.

I'm simply making the point that Jesus was explicit about the root of the problem. Heart trouble is the result of a troubled heart. The Greek *tarrasso* means 'agitated,' as in roiling water, like a de-masted ship in a hurricane. Remember, the agitated heart possibly harks way back to childhood.

Lets return to John 14. It ends the way it began, with Jesus repeating His opening words:

> John 14:27 *"Peace I leave with you, My peace I give to you; not as the world gives do I give to you. Let not your heart be troubled, neither let it be afraid."*

We're not to allow our heart to be troubled or afraid, but *how* do we achieve that enviable state of being? Jesus wants to teach us how. Meanwhile, Proverbs 17:22 informs us that a merry heart does good, like medicine. That includes a joyful attitude, a thankful attitude, a praising attitude...

Let's set off to discover this destination where we can live in the victory of fearlessness.

To repeat: in Luke 21:26 Jesus said unequivocally that the two causes of heart attacks are fear, and the (negative!) expectation of things to come. *Fear* is an emotion that deals with the present moment. It's about the adrenalin rush, it's an instant reaction to danger. *Expectation* is supposition concerning the future. We are supposed to have a confident expectation, based on the Word of God. The negative expectation that Jesus is referring to overlooks, overrides, or questions the Word and instead gazes steadily at the apparent circumstances, or economic forecasts, or doctor's prognosis - and helps produce the situation that creates fear.

Here's an illustration of the above point. Elvis Presley is reported to have said, when his mother died at forty-six years of age, that he wouldn't live past forty-six. He may not have lived in lifelong fear of that prediction, but he had an expectation of its fulfillment. He died of a heart attack when he was forty-two.

When we hear a prediction or prognosis that fails to acknowledge the Word of God, and we receive it into ourselves, we prepare the way for it to happen. Let's go back to John chapter 14, verse 1, and read again Jesus' prescription for leading a trouble-free life.

> *John 14:1 "Let not your heart be troubled; you believe in God, believe also in Me".*

Trouble-free is not the same as tribulation-free. *Tribulation* attacks from the outside. *Trouble* has to do with inner perception. Our hearts don't get tribulated, they get troubled - by tribulation. If we can understand the point Jesus is making here, we'll be able to live trouble-free in the midst of tribulation, fearless in the face of every threat that accosts us.

Our daily lives often feel as if we've been dumped in a mine field, and too often had one explode beneath us, searing nerves and 'troubling our heart,' to put it mildly.

It's clear from the above verse that it's necessary to believe both in God, but also specifically in Jesus. We'll get back to that, but let's read on. There's treasure hidden in this passage.

> John 14:2 *"In My Father's house are many mansions; if it were not so, I would have told you. I go to prepare a place for you."*

Hymns have been penned and sermons preached about the kind of houses Jesus is preparing for us in heaven. Yet *that is not what the scripture intends.* The Greek for 'house' literally means dwelling place. The verse is saying that there are many places where God dwells, many places where He makes Himself at home. Aren't we His temple? It is literally saying: 'In My Father's house the many will be indwelt.' 'The many' in biblical writings implies 'the all'. The verse means that all who dwell in the Father will be indwelt by Him, equally; not some more and some less. That's backed by several probably familiar scriptures:

> 1Co 3:16 *"Do you not know that you are the temple of God and that the Spirit of God dwells in you"?*

> 2Co 6:16 *"And what agreement has the temple of God with idols? For you are the temple of the living God. As God has said: "I WILL DWELL IN THEM AND WALK AMONG THEM. I WILL BE THEIR GOD, AND THEY SHALL BE MY PEOPLE."*

7

We're the dwelling place, and God is the inhabitant. It's not about Him building houses in Glory-land somewhere. But John 14:2 leads into verse 3, and we've been inclined to hitch the incorrect concept of a housing development to what comes next:

> John 14:3 *"And if I go and prepare a place for you, I will come again and receive you to Myself; that where I am, there you may be also."*

At some subconscious level we've imagined Jesus going through the agonies of the Cross so that He could get busy on His new calling in construction when He reached heaven. That seems to be what the bible is intimating. Instead, Jesus is talking about the benefits we'll derive because of the Father living in us, something which Jesus made possible. God didn't want to live behind a curtain or in a little box. He wanted to live inside us, He chose us as His dwelling. He wanted us to know the depth and magnitude of His love.

Firstly, Jesus told us that we, the "many mansions", are dwellings of the Father. Then He went on to say something about our future *because* the Father dwells in us. But because we've thought the verses were alluding to heaven, we've missed the point.

Over the years religion has devastated people by inferring that the bible is about heaven and hell. Certainly the bible mentions both, but heaven and hell are not the focus of redemption, as has been implied. The bible is about the love of God, the mercy of God, the grace of God extended to man specifically to empower mans life beginning in this world. It's about Father's desire for relationship and companionship, and the extent to which

8

He was prepared to go in order for us to be able to partake of the greatest blessing that could ever exist: life with Him now and evermore.

We've all read those seemingly ridiculous instructions on new appliances, like 'Do not submerge this hairdryer in water while it is plugged in', or, 'Do not touch the exhaust pipe while mower is running.' We chuckle, but the instructions are given because someone, somewhere, probably did those things. In the same way, God had to write about the hell that life would become for any man foolish enough to reject His love. They needed to know the results of that choice. And also that those who accepted His love would have a deeper understanding of how good their life was intended to be.

If heaven or hell were the focal point, then there would be only two important dates in our lives: that of our acceptance of Christ, and that of our graduation, when we're in a box and our family has to deal with our remains. It would reduce Jesus' awesome work to a one-dimensional accomplishment - the 'get 'em saved and get 'em home' mentality - and leave our intervening years draped in a mind-numbing fog of irrelevancy and uncertainty.

Jesus doesn't want us fumbling about in the fog, unsure of our direction in any given circumstance. He said. 'I go to prepare a place for you.' We need to lay a precise foundation for the voyage through the next few chapters, which means we have to get academic about Jesus' words. The Greek for 'place' is *topos*, which means: a spot, a condition, and an opportunity. Even in a single-dimensional understanding, that could mean heaven; but Jesus is saying much more.

Remember verse 1: "*Let not your heart be troubled.*" Again in verse 27, "*Let not your heart be troubled, neither let it be afraid.*" Jesus was preparing to eliminate fear and troubled hearts right then and there. He wasn't saying, "Let not your heart be troubled, because one day you'll be with Me in heaven." Instead He told them, "Let not your heart be troubled,   (now, today) because you are My Father's house, which means My Father dwells in each and every one of you, and knowing and believing that will remove all fear from you."

When Jesus said, "I go to prepare a place for you," He was referring to what He was about to do on the Cross. What did that mean? What was He going to do? Usually we think (not wrongly but incompletely) that He was going to die in our place and then rise again on the third day. True. But we live in such bondage to time that we think in 'three day potential': in other words, how much can one dead man accomplish in three days? We are carnally-minded, and as such are limited to the time-realm. That doesn't mean we're sinfully-minded; it means we're so focused on the things of the natural world that everything is confined to the elementary principles of this world. Thus: Jesus dies on the first day, lies in the tomb on the second and is raised on the third.

We fail to realize that when the natural body of Jesus of Nazareth expired on the Cross, then, because He was no longer bound by the limiting factors of physical existence, the timeless realm of eternity became His performance arena. He was consequently able to perform deeds from one end of eternity to the other - things that we have not imagined because we've been caught in the time-zone of thinking of His horrendous death and the imagined nothingness of the tomb-time.

10

Of course we acknowledge, because we've read it, He went to hell for us, became sin for us was raised on the third day. Nevertheless, in our minds we split this period into three twenty-four hour segments. But He had entered timeless eternity, and what He had to do He did in that realm, not here in ours.

Peter gives us some insight into this period in his first letter:

> *1Pe 3:18-19 "For Christ also suffered once for sins, the just for the unjust, that He might bring us to God, being put to death in the flesh but made alive by the Spirit, by whom also He went and preached to the spirits in prison"*

That scripture tells us that when Jesus was made alive by the Spirit He did two things, though at a glance we see only one because Peter put the first one earlier in the verse. He says that before Jesus went to preach to the imprisoned spirits, *He brought us to God.* He retrieved us and brought us to God.

Where were we then? Historically, we were non-existent. But because Jesus was outside time, in the realm of eternity, He went and laid hold of us and brought us to God. I say 'went' because of the sentence construction in verse 19: He 'also went' to the spirits in prison. That means He had 'went' somewhere else. He went first and brought us to God, then He also "went" to the spirits that Peter describes as having been disobedient back in Noah's days. He went there - in eternity. His body may have been lying dormant in a Jerusalem tomb, but His Spirit was fully occupied in eternal realms, securing humanity's peace, securing a trouble-free existence for us, as we shall see.

Naturally speaking all that covers a broad spectrum of time, as we would picture it. It's hard to bend our minds around Jesus drawing you and me, generations and centuries before we were born, and bringing us to the Father. In our terminology, He went forward in time, and He went back. In the timeless realm of eternity that's an illusory, non-existent issue. He went forward to our time, and all time from the Cross to the end of the ages, and brought us to the Father; and He went back to all time before the Cross and did the same, telling them that 'I am He of whom Noah spoke.' The bible shows that His words were heard for He 'led forth a host of captives'. (Eph. 4:8 NASV)

Hopefully we now realize that the days spent in the tomb had a mighty purpose. Jesus wasn't just lying around, dead, to pay our penalty - though that penalty of course had to be paid. The wages of sin were death, therefore He had to die. But the tomb-time was Jesus' release from the natural realm to make a journey from everlasting to everlasting, and thereby affect the events of the entire history of man. On our journey through the next chapters we'll discover why mankind, through the ages, has made so little use of what He did, has not understood it, and has not experienced it. But the purpose of this chapter is to lay a foundation of basic facts, from which to plot our course.

Every day of our life, yours, mine, and everybody's, present, past or future - in fact, every moment of all of our days - was affected by what Jesus did between the Cross and the resurrection. He went into every spot, every condition, and every opportunity of every situation in our lives and prepared it for our arrival before we got there. That means, He's already been here, where we are, facing today's Goliath! More than that: He wasn't here alone.

12

If we go to Strong's Concordance we'll see that 'I go to prepare a place for you' is an inaccurate translation. The Greek word *humin* doesn't mean 'for you'. It means 'with you, or by you.' 'For you' isn't an option. Jesus involved us. He literally went *with* each one of us to prepare a scenario with us. That's consistent with 'crucified *with* Him, buried *with* Him, raised *with* Him.' Back in the 1500s the translators couldn't wrap their brains around this concept - and it seems they still can't.

Jesus was saying to those around Him, "I'm taking you with Me now" (His "now", our then). He was saying the same thing to us. "I'm taking you with Me now (then) to make fully ready every spot you'll ever occupy, every condition you'll ever face, and every opportunity you'll ever have. I'm doing this so that when you get there historically, each spot, condition and opportunity will recognize *you* and know that you were with me when we were there before."

Because we haven't understood the implications of Jesus' words, we haven't been able to make use of them. How often have we said, "I'm in a tight spot," not knowing that Jesus has already been there? Jesus came with us to what we now imagine is a tight spot (it was probably much tighter when He first arrived!) and He made it big enough for us to squeeze in with Him and exercise a state of victory and success in it. It's not really a tight spot after all...

> John 14:3 *"And if I go and prepare a place for you, I will come again and receive you to Myself; that where I am, there you may be also."*

Let's expand on that verse in the light of what we've been discussing: *"If I go to prepare a spot, condition or*

13

opportunity with you, I will come again and receive you to Myself; so that where I am, there you may be also." Initially it looks as if Jesus is talking about His second coming and our new address in the new earth. Well, that's certainly involved, but it's not the exclusive interpretation. We've restricted so much of what Jesus has done for us through the love and grace of the Father, by exclusionary teachings such as those regarding the above verses.

Jesus will come again and take us to a new dimension, but that's not the intent behind His words in John 14. He talks about 'receiving' us to Himself. That's not the same word that is translated 'receive' when James 1:21 says, *"Receive the implanted word which is able to save your soul."* In that sentence, 'receive', *dechomai,* means to accept or take. In John 14: 3 the word used is *paralambano*; it means 'to associate with oneself, in any familiar or intimate act or relation.'

Jesus is the 'oneself'. Thus, "I will come again and associate you with Myself relationally in any familiar or intimate act." Or, more freely but still validly: "I will come again and identify you as Me, in every spot, condition and opportunity that you find yourself in."

Interestingly, in the next phrase 'where I am' can also be translated 'where I have been'. Therefore: "I will come again and identify you as Me in every spot, condition and opportunity that you find yourself in; that where I have been, there you may be also."

Regardless of any physical problem, economic distress or any tribulation that we may find ourselves in today, Jesus said we can be trouble-free and fearless, because He has already been there and brought His victory.

14

Let us not think that bearing our sickness and carrying our diseases happened only on the Cross. I believe rather that He went all the way through history, including the personal history of each person who ever lived, and dealt with every one of our failures and sicknesses and problems. He occupied and dealt with each and every spot, condition and opportunity we've ever faced or will face, all the failures and poverty and pain, and filled them all with victory and success. He's made it so that we can't fail there - if we really believe in God, and believe also in Him.

Now we begin to understand that 'believing in God and also in Him' includes believing in what He has said and done for us, as well as believing that He exists. The devils believe He exists, and they shudder. He's talking about something greater than believing that He is.

It gets better. Jesus continues, saying, *"I will receive you to (or unto) Myself."* Strong's tells us that this is a preposition of direction, toward and forward - not backward. "I will come again, identifying you as Me, causing you to move forward into the victory I've already achieved in this place."

These truths have changed my life. I now know that, no matter what I'm facing or how bad the situation looks, Jesus has been there with me, so that means the victory has been achieved - By Him, yes, but also by me, because He associated me with Him. When we encounter that circumstance, that cancer, that economic potential for failure, whatever it is, we need to understand that we've been there before, with Jesus, when He conquered the threat. Therefore this spot has been preconditioned for victory and is now favorable to us; the opportunity to succeed is available, so we can walk on through it, 'believing in God and in Jesus too' and see success unfold.

15

Jesus said, paraphrasing, "that where I am, having passed through the spots, conditions and opportunities of your life, you may be also."

Knowing that Jesus has been in every tribulation-spot of our life before we got there should change the way we see the situation. Knowing that He has made us victorious in it should do away with heart trouble and fear, and rather allow the peace that He has left for us to reign in our heart. But first we need to know it, and that's the destination we have in sight.

That's why Jesus said, "In the world you will have tribulation" - future tense - "but be of good cheer for I have overcome the world" - past tense.

Put in today's vernacular, Jesus said: 'Been there, done that, with you, before you - so don't sweat it.'

That's worth writing out, perhaps on the back of our checkbook!

There's one last scripture to add before closing this chapter. John chapter 13: 36:

John 13:36 Simon Peter said to Him, "Lord, where are You going?" Jesus answered him, "Where I am going you cannot follow Me now, but you shall follow Me afterward."

We think Jesus was alluding to two places: the grave, and heaven. "Where I am going you can't follow Me now, but you shall, afterward." But here we are, 2,000 years later, following where He's already been on our behalf and walking in the victory (more and more effectively as we understand it better) that He proclaimed and attained. And we're not in the grave or heaven yet.

Chapter 2

I Go Before You

One of the principle reasons for this journey is to move us away from the ingrained concepts of a heavenly future that we've picked up through religion - albeit so-called Christian religion (that's really an oxymoron: Christianity is neither a religion nor religious. It is a relationship with a living Person).

We've been taught about the wonderful hereafter awaiting us - all true! - but there's been too little mentioned about the wonderful here-and-now we're supposed to be enjoying, which God paid so highly to buy for us. Let's return to those first three verses of John 14, to examine them from a new perspective of expectation of success and victory, in every experience of every moment of every day.

Sadly, today's church seems to be composed of multitudes of amnesiacs who have forgotten who they are, and what God has bought for them. Consequently, many focus on the two dates mentioned in the previous chapter, the moment of accepting Christ and our death. The belief is instilled into us that we're saved so that we can go to heaven when we die. At least, that's how many of us were raised.

Because of this pervading mindset, we're going to look at a few more verses that back up this teaching that no matter what we have to face in our moment by moment life, Jesus has already been there, with us in Him, and brought it to a successful conclusion. In order to access that victory in whatever spot or circumstance we are facing, we need to be fully persuaded of this as truth. There are confirming scriptures throughout the bible, which we'll get to farther along.

To begin at the beginning: Adam in the Garden. Don't we believe that everything there was prepared to perfection *before* Adam arrived on the scene? Before he existed? Doesn't it make sense that the same thing happens in our individual cases? God went ahead and prepared a place for Adam, and did the same for us. The same kind of preparation and care was part of Christ's finished work.

We're told that we are a new creation. Just as everything had been prepared and designed for the old creation, so, too, for the new one. In a teaching entitled, 'Entering His Rest', I did an in-depth study on the two words 'very good' in verse 31 of Genesis 1:

> *Gen 1:31 Then God saw everything that He had made, and indeed it was very good.*

In a nutshell, those two words contain and include all the following: 'it' - everything He had made - was **'moving forward with great force, maintaining velocity, overcoming resistance, in order to be what He had made it to be.'** And then God rested. Why? Because what He had spoken had gone out and was continuing through time and eternity maintaining velocity, overcoming resistance and moving forward with great force, in order to be what He had commanded it to be.

That's why God doesn't have to get up on Sunday morning with a yawn and say, "Well, let there be sun." That's why He doesn't have to check out the stars and the moon at night. He said it once and it went forth from His mouth and prepared the entire future of the universe with one utterance.

Another example to consider is over in Genesis 17:5, where God says to Abram, "You shall be... for I have made..."

> "...but your name shall be Abraham; for I have made you a father of many nations".

God had put the word out from the foundation of the world that Abram would become Abraham, the father of many nations. Consequently, "you shall be... for I have made..." God had already prepared the spot, the condition and the opportunity, before Abraham arrived there historically.

Consider that spot and condition as he and Sarai approach it: his seed is dead within him; her ovaries are dead. They have a condition that will not allow them to produce children. But when the old couple arrive, they find that Jesus has already been there. Sarai's womb comes to life, as does Abram's seed.

Nothing has changed. This is a perfect illustration of what this book is describing, and of what Jesus was talking about in our scripture in John 14. But look, there's similar revelation in Paul's heart. It's Ephesians 1:5:

> Eph 1:5 " having predestined us to adoption as sons by Jesus Christ to Himself, according to the good pleasure of His will",

Some of us, perhaps most of us, have been taught that the above verse refers to who's going to accept Christ, or who's going to heaven or hell, and wars have been fought over it. But the verse has nothing to do with salvation. It's

19

about God predetermining that all of us would be His children - which is what we are as a result of what Jesus has done. Because we are in Jesus, the Son, we are all called 'sons'.

There are sons of obedience and sons of disobedience, as Ephesians 2:2 puts it:

> *"in which you once walked according to the course of this world, according to the prince of the power of the air, the spirit who now works in the sons of disobedience"*

Those who choose to reject all that Jesus offers are disobedient, but they are still sons - prodigal in their relationship with God, but sons. Look at verse 11:

> *Eph 1:11 "In Him also we have obtained an inheritance, being predestined according to the purpose of Him who works all things according to the counsel of His will,"*

It was predetermined that our destiny was to inherit God's estate. Before we drew our first breath, before we were seeds in our parents, before our parents existed, before everything, Jesus had already been here to create a spot and position for us to be God's sons, an opportunity for us to inherit His estate.

Similarly, before God placed Adam in the Garden He had prepared the spot and condition, had 'stocked the pantry' for Adam. The very name 'Eden' is a word that underlines that. It's not a postal address or geographical place, given so that we could find it on a map; it's a description, a name that encompasses its essence: a place of pleasure, of soft, comfortable, delightful, voluptuous living - a name God chose, not Adam.

God has never asked or expected anybody to do anything alone, for any period of time, ever. He is a go-before-us Father. Let's look at Isaiah 45: 2-3:

> *Isa 45:2-3 "I will go before you And make the crooked places straight; I will break in pieces the gates of bronze And cut the bars of iron. I will give you the treasures of darkness And hidden riches of secret places, That you may know that I, the LORD, Who call you by your name, Am the God of Israel."*

God says *He* will go, *He* will break, *He* will cut, and then *He* will give us the treasures and riches. That looks as if He's been there, done that for us... It's consistent with Jesus' words: that He'll go before us to prepare a place for us, that He'll go to make, break and cut. He'll pre-pare,(pare things before), so that when we get there, if we know it, then the treasures and the riches will be available and waiting for us. That doesn't mean just dollars and cents, but wholeness and completion in every aspect of our lives. Isaiah 52 backs this up:

> *Isa 52:12 "For you shall not go out with haste, Nor go by flight; For the LORD will go before you, And the God of Israel will be your rear guard."*

The word 'haste' in the Hebrew speaks of trepidation, of hurrying in fear. God tells us through the above passage that since He has already gone into the situation (or the diagnosis from the doctor or divorce lawyer, etc) before us and prepared it, there is no need to fear or flee. The New King James uses the words 'rear guard' for what the old King James translates strangely as 'rereward'. It actually means to gather or receive us to Himself. The sentence could read, 'The Lord will go before you and gather you or receive you to Himself.'

If those words sound familiar, perhaps it's because we are remembering Jesus saying in John 14:3 that He will go to prepare a place for us and then come again and receive us to Himself. He will draw us into the victory He has already created for us - by having already been where we now are. When we understand this, and accept it, the many problems life throws up at us will seem less difficult. These days my wife and I experience far more resistance, persecution and hardship than ever before, but it is much easier to deal with now. Circumstances that would have flattened us thirty years ago are able to be turned around. It's about being trouble-free in the middle of the problem.

It has always been the Father's way to go ahead, prepare a place - and then bring us to it. It's important to understand that what Jesus said is based on the Father's love relationship with mankind from the beginning. Look at Exodus 23:20:

> *Ex. 23:20 "Behold, I send an Angel before you to keep you in the way and to bring you into the place which I have prepared."*

God always goes ahead of us to prepare a place where we can live sumptuously and voluptuously and delightfully. Notice He says, "to keep you in the way". That means to guard and protect us. We are kept, protected and guarded by the faith of Jesus Christ. The Hebrew word 'way' - *derek* - means course of life. The word for 'place,' *maqom*, means exactly the same - opportunity, place and condition. He goes ahead to prepare an opportunity, condition and location for us, but note: 'to bring you into the place which

I have prepared'. Not a place which *we* have prepared. Look at Deuteronomy, chapter 6:

> *Deut 6:10-12 "So it shall be, when the LORD your God brings you into the land of which He swore to your fathers, to Abraham, Isaac, and Jacob, to give you large and beautiful cities which you did not build, houses full of all good things, which you did not fill, hewn-out wells which you did not dig, vineyards and olive trees which you did not plant—when you have eaten and are full—then beware, lest you forget the LORD who brought you out of the land of Egypt, from the house of bondage".*

In verse 6, 'when' shows that this is a future-tense statement. God will prepare 'beautiful cities which they will not have built, houses full of good things not provided by them, wells dug for them, vineyards and olive groves planted by others.' Now let's read Joshua 24: 11-13 to see the flip-side of this, looking back instead of forward (bold-type mine):

> *Josh 24:11-13 "Then you went over the Jordan and came to Jericho. And the men of Jericho fought against you—also the Amorites, the Perizzites, the Canaanites, the Hittites, the Girgashites, the Hivites, and the Jebusites. But I delivered them into your hand. I sent the hornet before you which drove them out from before you, also the two kings of the Amorites, but **not with your sword or with your bow**. I have given you a land **for which you did not labor**, and cities **which you did not build**, and you dwell in*

*them; you eat of the vineyards and olive groves **which you did not plant.** "* (Emphasis mine)

God made it clear to them, in case they needed reminding, that their victories and the spoils of war that they were enjoying were all His doing, not a result of their efforts. Now to Genesis 15:13-16:

> *Gen 15:13-16 Then He said to Abram: "Know certainly that your descendants will be strangers in a land that is not theirs, and will serve them, and they will afflict them four hundred years. And also the nation whom they serve I will judge; afterward they shall come out with great possessions. Now as for you, you shall go to your fathers in peace; you shall be buried at a good old age. But in the fourth generation they shall return here, for the iniquity of the Amorites is not yet complete."*

For four hundred years, God had other peoples developing a place for Abraham's descendants, so that when they returned to Israel, everything would be ready and waiting for them. They could move into cities and houses they didn't build, eat from olive trees and vineyards they didn't plant, drink from wells they didn't dig. And by the way, I'm not advocating that you go over to your neighbor's house expecting to take over his possessions!

Psalm 105:42-44 confirms what I've been writing.

> *Ps 105:42-44 "For He remembered His holy promise, And Abraham His servant. He brought out His people with joy, His chosen*

ones with gladness. He gave them the lands of the Gentiles, And they inherited the labor of the nations"

God arranged for another nation to labor for four hundred years preparing a country for the Israelites. Then He sent hornets before the Israelites to drive out the inhabitants, so that there would be no need to fight, or even lift a sword or a bow.

This is exactly what Jesus is talking about. He's gone before us, like a hornet, neutralizing all the harmful aspects in everything that would come against us when we get to those cities that we didn't build and houses filled with good things that we didn't buy. Those places will recognize us as the rightful owners of the property when we arrive because we were with Him and in Him the first time He went there. With this picture in mind, let's visit still another scripture, the well-known Jeremiah 29:11:

> *Jer 29:11 "For I know the thoughts that I think toward you, says the LORD, thoughts of peace and not of evil, to give you a future and a hope".*

'Thoughts' can equally be translated 'plans, intentions or purposes'. Thus, 'I know the plans I have or devise for you, thoughts and plans of peace, to give you a future and a hope.' 'Peace' *shalom*, is a big, powerful word. It encapsulates safety, wellness/health, prosperity, happiness, wholeness. In Joseph Prince's book, "Unmerited Favor", he uses an entire paragraph to cover all *shalom's* meanings.

The King James version of this scripture translates 'to give you a future and a hope' as: 'to give you an expected end.' The phrase literally means 'a cord or an attachment to the future.' The innate intention and sense of this verse is that all the safety and happiness and prosperity God provides for us in the present is also our ongoing connection to the future, so that when we arrive we'll discover that He has already been there and secured our spot, position and opportunity of safety, wellness, prosperity and happiness.

It's important to know what to look for, **to have an expectation** of *shalom* based on God's Word to each of us individually. Expectation is a form of trust; we know from John 14:1-3 that we can and should have an expectation that Jesus has already been to our present and future situations and prepared them for our arrival. I'd like to have t-shirts made that say in bold print: **"Been there, done that, with you, before you - so don't sweat it!"** and have them signed **'Jesus'**.

If we don't know what to expect and we're not looking for it, well, we have a dependable adversary prowling about like a roaring lion in wait for those who are ignorant of who they are and of their previously prepared victory over and in every situation. He gets us the same old way every time - through ignorance, because he can't touch us any other way - he's defeated, stripped of all power, a washout. He can't affect us unless we permit him to do so through our ignorance of his true standing. He's the same smooth-talking operator he always has been, a liar, a deceiver. But power? He has none. Authority? None. Jesus sorted all that out two thousand years ago. There's no need to be afraid of Satan. Rather, be aware of his craftiness in painting the picture hopeless when it isn't, and of coloring himself scary instead of the pathetic loser he is.

If we're unaware of our protected and victorious stand-ing in Jesus, we'll be misled into defeat. We'll think like the world, agreeing with what the circumstances are saying: "Well, if the 'flu is coming to town I'd better get my 'flu shot." Or, "Well, the stock market is falling, I'd better sell." Our decisions shouldn't be based on popular opinion but on God's promises and trustworthiness.

If we haven't seen the victory in our situations, maybe it's because we haven't had an expectation, a personal expectation based on His Word to us: "Believe in God; believe also in Me. I go to prepare a place for you." We need to understand and know that He has already gone into every situation we're facing and will ever face, and filled it with His power and glory and greatness.

To end this chapter, let's go to a last, confirming example to identify a 'type' of Jesus, found in Joseph, the preeminent son of Jacob/Israel's old age. Genesis 37: 3:

> *Gen 37:3 "Now Israel loved Joseph more than all his children, because he was the son of his old age."*

Accepting that Joseph is a type of Christ, look at Genesis 45:4-5:

> *Gen 45:4-5 And Joseph said to his brothers, "Please come near to me." So they came near. Then he said: "I am Joseph your brother, whom you sold into Egypt. But now, do not therefore be grieved or angry with yourselves because you sold me here; **for God sent me before you to preserve life.**"* (Emphasis mine)

God sent Joseph, a type of Jesus, ahead of his brothers to make provision for them. Now go to verses 7, 11, 18 and 26:

27

Gen 45:7   "And God sent me before you to preserve a posterity for you in the earth, and to save your lives by a great deliverance."

Gen 45:11 " There I will provide for you, lest you and your household, and all that you have, come to poverty; for there are still five years of famine."

Gen 45:18   "Bring your father and your households and come to me; I will give you the best of the land of Egypt, and you will eat the fat of the land."

Gen 45:26   And they told him [Jacob], saying, "Joseph is still alive, and he is governor over all the land of Egypt."

Remember, for 'Joseph,' read 'Jesus': Jesus is still alive and is Governor over all the land!

The final scripture is Genesis 50:20:

Gen 50:20 " But as for you, you meant evil against me; but God meant it for good, in order to bring it about as it is this day, to save many people alive".

No matter what we're facing at any and every moment of our physical lives, if we are going to access our victory in Jesus we need to know and believe that He has been in that moment and brought it to a successful conclusion. Jesus went from end to end of the timeless realm of eternity and into all of everyone's moments, during His three days between the Cross and resurrection. He wants us to be aware that we can approach the spots and opportunities and conditions and experiences of our lives, with a new

28

understanding, with expectancy and confidence, and with a fearless and untroubled heart.

Jesus never indicated that we wouldn't have to face negative conditions and situations. Rather, He said we *would* experience them. But He made a way for us to be trouble-free in the midst of tribulation, a way for our heart to be strong. It happens by knowing that we have already been there together, us and Him: He's been there, done that, with us, before us!

Chapter 3

The Language of Eternity

As we'll be studying John 14:1-3 in more depth in this chapter, let's examine it on our chart:

> *John 14:1 "Let not your heart be troubled; you believe in God, believe also in Me. In My Father's house are many mansions; if it were not so, I would have told you. I go to prepare a place for you. And if I go and prepare a place for you, I will come again and receive you to Myself; that where I am, there you may be also".*

We've seen previously that a troubled heart - stress, worry, fears - can and often does manifest problems in the physical realm, in our actual, physiological heart. In the first three verses of John 14, Jesus describes a way of life that is heart-trouble free even when trouble marches in like an invading army. Maybe in the past we initially put up some resistance, but when the heavy artillery moved in we surrendered, taken captive by the overwhelming, insurmountable odds against us. That's what Jesus is talking about. Now He offers a way to live fearlessly, to be a secure fortress that can be neither occupied nor dominated by anything we have to face.

This doesn't mean we won't come under attack—rather, we're guaranteed to experience it, by Jesus Himself (to paraphrase): "In this world you'll have tribulation - but relax! There's a place you can live in where the worst that can come against won't be able to affect you, a place I've prepared you, for I've overcome the world."

A troubled heart is an inside response to an outside influence. Jesus starts off by telling us He has information that will protect our hearts from being imprisoned by the enemy, tortured with anxiety, sleeplessness, stress, nervousness, and, always lurking somewhere along the twisting corridors of our mind, fear.

The focus of this chapter is on developing more fully the concept of the preparation - or preconditioning - of the locations, conditions and opportunities of our lives. In order to understand Jesus' words in verse 2 about going to prepare a place for us, we'll have to grasp biblical language that speaks to us from outside of time, though we are used to reading the bible 'inside' time.

The words we read on the pages of the bible generally speak to us from inside of time, dealing with the realm in which we live. There is another biblical language, though, which speaks to us from outside of time, from eternity into our timed existence. It's a language that isn't bound by the things with which we measure our lives in this physical bubble that exists in the limitless timelessness of eternity. Assessments of time and distance are subordinate expressions of the greater spiritual reality.

When Peter tried to explain this concept to the people of the first century, he used Psalm 90:4 as a springboard: "a day with the Lord is as a thousand years". He wasn't intending that anyone take that literally and start working out how long the seven days of creation might be, but was illuminating a concept of timelessness. He was enticing their minds to stretch beyond the natural realm and glimpse something else altogether, a sphere where a thousand years was a synonym for maybe a million or a billion in today's world of big figures. He was helping them envisage eternity.

We are not (as is often believed) physical beings who attend Sunday church for a spiritual experience. We are spiritual beings living a constant physical experience. That physical experience is nevertheless spiritual in every way, because our physical bodies were created by the Spirit God. Our indwelling personal presence is our spirit, so everything about us physically is truly spiritual, though this manifests within the confines of time and distance.

Consequently, we consider everything - healing, prosperity, bible reading - from a natural perspective of measurements and limitations (time and distance). If something happened, it is in the past, unless it is still encroaching on the present. We're not practiced in seeing future events completed, relegated to the past, and yet still waiting our arrival. That doesn't fit into our time-line vision.

The scripture speaks often in a language that reveals the timeless influence of eternity - or the influence of timeless eternity - on those events that are still to be manifest in our life, that are still future for us. Yet it speaks of those things as already having been accomplished, already prepared and preconditioned for our arrival, so when we get there we can have a kick-butt attitude! When we have that attitude our heart is not troubled. It makes no difference what comes up against us, we know who has been there already, and who was with Him when He was there. We know He identifies Himself with us, identifies us as Him - and we find the problem is under our feet.

We need to recognize and become familiar with biblical language that speaks to us outside of time and into time.

> *Heb 10:1 For the law, having a shadow of the good things to come, and not the very image of the things,*
>
> *Heb 8:5 who serve the copy and shadow of the heavenly things, as Moses was divinely instructed when he was about to make the tabernacle. For He said, "SEE THAT YOU MAKE ALL THINGS ACCORDING TO THE PATTERN SHOWN YOU ON THE MOUNTAIN."*

Paul says in 2 Cor. 4:18 that "the things that are seen are temporary, but the things that are not seen are eternal." 'Heavenly things' in Hebrews 8:5, above, refers to eternal things. Eternal things are not affected by time and distance. Paul refers to a copy of the heavenly things. If we try to make a copy of a letter, using a copy machine, we can push the start button all we want but if there's no letter in the copier, it's not going to make a copy. There has to be a preexisting substance of reality before it can be copied.

Also mentioned in verse 5 is, the 'shadow of heavenly things'. If we tie it up to chapter 10, verse 1, the heavenly things are 'good things to come.' A shadow can't be cast by nothing, there first has to be something there, something of an existing substance. And although the thing in verse 5 is still to come, it is casting a shadow. Therefore, as far as time goes, the thing was in the future - but eternally speaking, it was already preexisting.

When we think of eternity, we usually don't see in our mind's eye that whole realm out there which is responsible for the manifestation in this realm. We rather envision a lo-o-o-ong time, how lo-o-ong we're going to be with God, or how lo-o-o-ng He's been around; and we understand that we can't put a limitation on either. But most of us don't picture an enormous world beyond the confines of our imagination, filled with marvelous 'stuff'. Similarly, our body is the physical extension of the true person. When our body drops off, our spirit leaves, set free to be much more alive than it was when it was stuffed into the little tube of clay that is our physical self!

Back to the shadows of heavenly things. Shadows are created by light from beyond a substance shining across it. With that in mind, look at Colossians 2:16-17:

> *Col 2:16-17 " So let no one judge you in food or in drink, or regarding a festival or a new moon or sabbaths, which are a shadow of things to come, but the substance is of Christ."*

I studied this out because it didn't sound right. Paul always tries to distance us from any connection to the Law, yet here he says the Laws 'are' a shadow. Once again, it is the translators who are at fault. The sense is that the shadow 'was' of the things that 'have come', because the substance that casts the shadow is of Christ.

Let's explore these waters a little. Revelation 13:8 tells us that Christ is the Lamb slain from the foundation of the world. Christ is the substance casting the shadow. To the Israelites in the desert receiving the Law, the foundation of the world was in the past. Yet the Law was a shadow of things to come - historically speaking, a future event, yet one that had already happened. There in the wilderness of Sinai they were seeing a shadow that was being cast from the future back into time by a light on the other side, and the light on the other side was and is the eternal revelation of God.

Once this time-eternity-future-present-past concept is grasped, it should stimulate a consciousness that will allow us to meet every day, every spot, every condition and every opportunity that we have yet to encounter with the confidence that this moment has already been prepared and made ready for us, to be a success regardless of how it looks as we walk into it.

It's easy in theory, but when that diagnosis of pancreatic cancer or inoperable brain tumor is spoken over us, it can be tough in practice. That's why we're on this voyage - so that in that moment, you can know that you have a choice to make. Whether you choose to go with the diagnosis or not, God will still love you. But you have an opportunity as well, to recognize that Jesus has already been there with you from time immemorial; He has already prepared this moment for you to go face-to-face with it and for you to be the top-dog, the confident victor!

Hebrews 11:13, speaking of the elders and heroes of Israelite history, says: *'These all died in faith, not having received the promises, but having seen them afar off were assured {*the word means persuaded*} of them, embraced them and confessed that they were strangers and pilgrims on the earth'*...

'Seeing the promises' - the word 'seeing', *eido*, means to be aware, to perceive, to understand. It doesn't necessarily indicate that they had a little movie reel in their mind actually showing all the processes we're going to talk about. It means they were aware, or perceived, that they could take the experiences and communication they'd had with the Father, and from these perceive the future. If we read carefully, that's backed up by the above scripture. The verse refers to the visual acuity of people who were **not** bound by a time and distance reality, who understood that time and distance were part of God's greater plan, that 'this' is not all there is, isn't the end of it, and isn't even where it comes from.

What promises did they see 'from afar off'? Scriptures written in a book? A small box of promise cards on someone's coffee table? I don't mean to mock, but I have a problem with people who talk incessantly about the Promises of God, because a promise is something that hasn't yet been fulfilled. Meanwhile, they have all been fulfilled in and by Jesus, and are now a reality.

The Israelites of verse 13 saw the promises afar off. They were perceiving the finished work of Christ and all it encompassed - hence the plural, promises. 2 Corinthians 1:20 says, "*In Christ, all the promises of God are Yes and Amen*" - which means: finalized, done, no longer promises but realities!!! So if we are 'standing on the promises', we are living in the Old Covenant. I grew up singing a hymn on Sundays about "Standing on the promises of Christ my King through eternal ages". We need no longer stand on promises, but on the fulfillment of promises!

Those old heroes saw the finished work of the Cross and all it contained. 'From afar' is not a distance measurement. It means is they perceived things finished in the eternal realm, but not yet accomplished in time, so they saw them afar off in the sense that they perceived things from out in eternity - outside of time and distance. They also saw them as being unfulfilled yet in that time afar off. See how that works? So there wasn't any time or distance limitation.

To repeat, I am not saying that they watched these things played out as in a movie theater, but they saw the Cross, the Resurrection, the Ascension and the Return, because they saw the finished work of Jesus and all it contained. They obviously saw the new heavens and the new earth, because 'they understood themselves to be strangers and pilgrims (the words mean aliens and foreigners) on the earth.' They must have had a perception of the new heaven and the new earth as a part of the full picture of the finished work of Jesus Christ. It says that they were persuaded of and embraced the promises, which means they were persuaded of *the future preparation of the finished work of the Lord Jesus.*

Another example of eternity in time is given by Jesus in John 8:56. He said, *"Your father Abraham rejoiced to see My day, and he saw it and was glad."* Neither Abraham nor the heroes of Hebrews 11 saw a collection of scriptures written in a book for a far-off future time - yet that's how we view them 2,000 years later, even now waiting for the promises to come to pass at some still-to-happen moment. We're taught to believe Him 'for' this or that, although He's already 'done' it all. How much longer are we going to stay blinded by teachings that overlook or negate the finished work of Christ?

All the territory under the Lordship of Jesus has been prepared to our advantage, outside of time, before time, and then inserted back into time, for the experience of those who will see it, be persuaded of it, and embrace it. And while we're on the subject, let's define what Jesus' territory of Lordship includes:

Mat 28:18 And Jesus came and spoke to them, saying, "All authority has been given to Me in heaven and on earth."

38

This isn't referring to the heaven where God sits on His throne with Jesus, this means the heavenly places that so many Christians worry about, imagining that this is where demons dwell and plan ways to torment Christians' daily lives. Here's what goes on there: **nothing**, because Jesus is Lord of the heavens and the earth. So I repeat: All of the territory of the Lordship of Jesus, which we have just defined - all the heavens and all the earth - that territory has been prepared to our advantage, outside of time, before time and now has been fitted into time for the experience of those who will see it, be persuaded of it and embrace it.

We can reject this message and continue to greet each spot, condition and opportunity with trepidation, worldly expectation and fear, and if we do we'll never know that Jesus was there with us and before us. Then we'll say, "When I was in that situation it was obviously not prepared for me." Why? Because we didn't stand up in the face of that situation and say, "Ha, ha! I know something that you don't know." But the situation does know it, because it was visited by Jesus many years ago and it recognizes you as having been with Him, and awaits your authoritative proclamation.

The situation is still under the manipulative control of the god of this world, but the god of this world is under our feet. He goes about seeking whom he may devour, seeking someone who doesn't believe and know this, seeking someone too timid to declare the victory of Christ from ages past. Then he can greet that person with a circumstance that will become his end.

The evidence we have in the church today is that this can't possibly be true. We think that "I go to prepare a place for you" must refer to heaven, because we've never met that cancer or this financial ruin or any other thing head on and declared that Jesus had already been there. Jesus had nothing to do with the cancer - He went into every situation that we experience and says, "I have already gone in and cleansed it, purified it, and made it what you need it to be in order to enjoy victory, success and peace of heart. Let not your hearts be troubled, neither let them be afraid." Why did He say those words? Because "in the last days, men's hearts will fail them for fear and the expectation of things to come" - like a 3 to 6 months prognosis.

Isaiah 45 confirms our need to confront the spots and conditions with this revelation.

> *Isa 45:21 "Tell and bring forth your case; Yes, let them take counsel together. Who has declared this from ancient time? Who has told it from that time? Have not I, the LORD? And there is no other God besides Me, A just God and a Savior; There is none besides Me."*

"Who has declared this from ancient time?" 'This' would refer to the condition or situation that Israel was experiencing at that moment, as would 'it' in the following sentence. Here's what it looks like when we use the vernacular of this book: "Who has declared this spot, this condition, this moment from ancient time? Who has told it (the spot. condition, moment) from that time? Have not I, the Lord?"

God had declared from way back in their historical past what He had already prepared for this moment. In John 14:2-3 Jesus is telling us what He has prepared for the now-situation that we face. His words don't allude to just the moment of His physical return to earth, though that is

40

included. From ancient time He has been declaring the Lamb slain from the foundation of the world. From ancient time He has been declaring 'this', 'it', this moment, this spot, this condition. That doesn't mean He arranged the negative circumstance. Rather, He announced the victory over it, which is the point He's making and His word to us is "Tell and bring forth your case"

Again in Isaiah 46:10 God speaks of Himself:

> *Isa 46:10 "Declaring the end from the beginning, And from ancient times things that are not yet done"*

"Declaring from the beginning"...and then again (let's drop the word 'declaring down a line to follow the context), "Declaring from ancient times things that are not yet done."

God is describing 'things' that have not yet happened in our historical experience, but have nevertheless been completed from ancient times. They are the stuff of our 'now-moment', the assured presence of Christ and His victory over every second of our lives, as He enjoys both the good times with us and His triumph over the bad. He has been in every one of our moments, before us and with us in Him, cleansing, purifying and perfecting them so that when we arrive there historically we can enjoy victory, success and peace of heart.

If we can arrive in all the nanoseconds of our life with a sense of trust in Christ's victory in them, we'll discover that our attitude is the key that opens the door to their manifestation.

> *Isa 48:5 Even from the beginning I have declared it to you; Before it came to pass I proclaimed it to you, Lest you should say,*

> *'My idol has done them, And my carved image and my molded image Have commanded them.'*

Couldn't that be paraphrased to say, "Before it became your experience, my Word was already in the moment"? And, "All the things you have already experienced - the former things, everything that's happened, everything you've witnessed - I announced them to you from the beginning, before your time." In verse 3 God had said, *"I have declared the former things from the beginning; They went forth from My mouth, and I caused them to hear it. Suddenly I did them, and they came to pass."*

The word 'suddenly', *pithom*, means instantly, but not as in, "I did it suddenly yesterday." The sense is rather that of an instant of a release, as in Genesis 1:31: *Then God saw everything that He had made, and indeed it was very good.* Remember, the words rendered 'very good' in English, mean in the original Hebrew, "moving with great force – maintaining velocity, overcoming resistance in order to be what God had commanded it to be. Everything is continuing because that is what He commanded it to do in a moment of expended, spoken energy.

"Suddenly I did them, and they came to pass", could equally be rendered, "I did them instantaneously, but they came to pass in your time." The former things that He had declared were first spoken by Him, and then made to **hear** their intended purpose, place and time. They couldn't happen in just sometime or anytime - they were for a specific purpose and place; they had a time-target, and God never misses the bull's-eye.

> *Ecc 3:1" To everything there is a season, a time for every purpose under heaven:"*

42

King Solomon is using his own turn of phrase to convey the same information as the prophet Isaiah. Look at the words, "under heaven". If there is an 'under heaven', there must obviously also be a heaven. Time is associated with the under heaven arena, not with heaven. Ecclesiastes is here contrasting time and eternity. If we look into this we find that the under-heaven realm is already prepared with purposed things. The word 'purpose', *chephetz,* means 'pleasurable, delightful and desirable'! *"To everything there is a season, a time for every pleasurable, delightful and desirable thing under heaven."*

The 'under heaven' is already prepared with pleasurable, delightful and desirable things purposed by God's heart. Wherever we go - this step, that place, everywhere - is intended by God to be a new Eden. Eden is the epitome of biblical demonstration of what God purposed for our lives. We learned earlier that 'Eden' was a word used by the ancient Hebrews to express 'pleasurable, delightful, voluptuous living'.

> *Ecc 3:11 He has made everything beautiful in its time.*

'He has made' is past tense. Again we experience this language that speaks from eternity into our lives, telling us that God has prepared time for our pleasure and success and victory. **He has scheduled a progressive unfolding of His grace in each and every season on our life.** One of the Hebrew definitions of grace includes pleasure, delight and favor. This what He has scheduled for *every season* of our life.

The sense of progressive unfolding means that there is no stagnation in God's plans for us, not even when we're at a good place - because He has a better place around the next corner of time. That's not supposed to make us greedy or dissatisfied. It's to help us understand what the bible means when it says in 1 Cor 2:9: *"Eye has not seen, nor ear heard, nor have entered to the heart of man the things which God has prepared for those who love Him."* God is telling us not to become content to stay even on the best plateau!

I'll illustrate this with a personal example. I remember how happy and excited I was when I found out that every time Marilyn and I laid hands on our little children- 37 years ago - they got healed. That was great! About two years later we both began to get restless about the fact that they were still getting the fevers. We'd pray for them and healing would always manifest, but we began to feel we shouldn't be content on that plateau, though it was wonderful, but Jesus didn't die so that our kids could be sick and then get healed. He died for their health!

It's that way with everything in life: we shouldn't be content in the sense of being satisfied to stay there forever. God has a progressive unfolding of grace already scheduled in our life for every season, every day of our natural experience. Each spot, condition and opportunity has been preloaded and customized to provide pleasure, delight and favorable regard to the bearer on demand.

We find out from Romans 8:19 that there is a proviso. "The creation eagerly waits for the revealing of the sons of God" The unfolding drama of delightful God-intended provision is for those who will embrace it with expectation. It is this concept, this idea that God has a progressive unfolding of revelation, that should draw us and never let us quit wanting to know all of Him that we can know, before we pass from this physical life. Let's desire to experience everything He has for us, realizing there is no

44

end to the revelation that we can experience on earth (at least until He returns, when we'll know Him as we are known).

When the bible says God has made everything beautiful in its time that includes the ugly circumstances that rumble like enemy tanks into our unsuspecting life. They won't stop crushing us under their weight of misery and stress and will remain detrimental until we're fully persuaded of, and embrace in faith, what God has already done in the spots and conditions that are attacking us. When we change our perspective and stand on the certainty of Jesus' visit to, and conquest over, our situation, then the victory is released.

When we encounter beautiful and pleasing circumstances let's be quick to rejoice and be grateful, thanking God that things are going well, and for all his benefits. The emphasis of this book is to help us get through the rough times, intact and victorious!

In Ecclesiastes 3 we need to deal with a mistranslation of the remainder of verse 11. It has been rendered, *'Also He has put eternity in their hearts, **except that** no one can find out the work that God does from beginning to end.'* The original Hebrew doesn't mean *'except that'*, but rather, *'without which.'* That alters the meaning significantly to:

*Ecc 3:11 " He has made everything beautiful in its time. Also He has put eternity in their hearts, **without which** no one can find out the work that God does from beginning to end."*

Apparently God wants us to find out the work that He has done from the beginning to cover us from beginning to end, so He put eternity in our heart - because without it we can't discover what He has done for us.

45

The mistake in translation reflects the translators' theological bent, which is a doctrine that permeates the church until today: that we can't know what our Sovereign God has in store for us, if He will or wants to heal, or give, or move in any matter. Jesus came to show us His will and make it possible for it to be applied - and it's always good.

God has put eternity in our heart because He wants us to know what He has planned for our future. He wants us to know that He has preconditioned and made it ready for us, so that when we get there it won't surprise us or set us back. We will be able to walk through it, the fire and flood, unscathed.

Eternity in our heart means, He has put the capacity inside our heart for understanding and experiencing everything He has accomplished for us in Time, while outside of Time. He has put the future He prepared for us, in our heart, waiting to be released by our words of faith and heart of faith in His finished work. As Ecclesiastes continues in verse 12, *"I know that nothing is better for them than to rejoice, and to do good in their lives."*

That's the way to embrace the finished work of Jesus: with persuasion and rejoicing.

Ecc 3:15 "That which is has already been, and what is to be has already been;"

Whoa! There it is, a gem to hold in our hearts, to be examined often in the sunlight of God's love. We can know that both present and future have been prepared for us by our amazing God. There is no need for fear or trepidation ever again, for victory over every negative worldly prognosis is ours for the taking - it has been given, and like salvation, waits only for us to exercise our ownership by accepting and believing, and then experiencing it. It is not something to earn - it is simply our inheritance. Isaiah sums it up succinctly in Chapter 54:17 of his book:

> *"No weapon formed against you shall prosper, and every tongue which rises against you in judgment You shall condemn. This is the heritage of the servants of the LORD, and their righteousness is from Me,"* *Says the LORD.*

Chapter 4

Somewhere in Your Future

We understand that the bible is divided by Jesus' life, death and resurrection into two sections: the Old Testament or Covenant, and the New Testament/Covenant. Because we accept that both Testaments are God-breathed, God-inspired, we therefore often accept what is written in both as being equally pertinent. We have seldom been taught to shine the light of the finished work of the Cross and Jesus' fulfillment of the Mosaic Law, onto the pre-Cross period, and in that glorious luminosity to see almost every line of the Old Testament from a new vantage point that changes the shape, intention and impact of what we're reading.

An example of this anomaly is that in the Old Testament epoch, God's visitations to and anointing of people were infrequent. We think of Moses, David, Samuel and the prophets; it was on such that the other Israelites had to depend to hear God's words and will. However, since Jesus' death, burial, resurrection and ascension, *we* are now the dwelling place of the Spirit of God. His presence is no longer an occasional phenomenon.

Perhaps because we still have a partial Old Testament mindset, when we read Jesus' words in John 14 about mansions in the Father's house and going to prepare a place for us, we assume, without thinking it through, that He is talking about one single destination, one final resting place: heaven. The entire theme of this book is about showing that supposition to be far too narrow.

Let's refresh our memories with another look at Jesus' words:

> *John 14:2-3 " In My Father's house are many mansions; if it were not so, I would have told you. I go to prepare a place for you. And if I go and prepare a place for you, I will come again and receive you to Myself; that where I am, there you may be also."*

We've seen that 'place', *topos*, means 'spot, location, or opportunity'. What also caught my attention though, is the word 'again', *palin,* which, according to Strong's definition, refers to 'an oscillatory repetition'. That's another way of saying, 'repeatedly coming again.' Repeatedly means more than once or twice! And the word 'receive' is equally interesting, meaning 'associate with'. So: "I will come repeatedly and associate Myself with you, or identify you as Me; that where I am, there may you be also." That's powerful.

Paul gave us a similar concept when he said, "It is no longer I who live, but Christ lives in me," in Galatians 2:20. He continued that revelation in Philippians1:21: "For me to live is Christ." Paul understood that he had been so fully associated with Christ that he had been given the same identity. In the same vein, John wrote in 1 John 4:17: "As He is, so also are we in this world."

So Jesus is saying, "If I go and prepare for you the locations, the conditions and the opportunities of life, I will come repeatedly and I will associate you with Me - I will identify you as Me in those situations, as you encounter them in life." Alternatively, that means, "Where I am, or where I exist or have been, you will be also." Wherever He has been, He has been victorious. Wherever He has been

He has been successful. That's why the scripture can tell us He is now seated at the right-hand of God, having finished the work, having perfected for all time those who are being sanctified. Us!

We will **never** encounter any situation that has not been long ago preconditioned in our favor by a visit from Jesus. Once the anchor of that thought is embedded deeply in our mind, we can face whatever the future holds, and we can anticipate it with a sense of expectation, knowing we have the victory over anything that rises up against us.

I'm not saying that Jesus sends the circumstances, the diseases and accidents and disappointments, though the Church's twisted doctrine of God's sovereignty might lead us to think that. He did not and will not ordain such things - instead He sent Jesus to redeem us from the curse of the Law, to die for us and set us free. I *am* saying that He has prepared everything to have a favorable outcome for us. I'm saying that Jesus did a work in these circumstances and conditions of life, so that when we arrive there and acknowledge His preparedness, the circumstances will bow to us and we will find the favor of God in them. The Bible does not say that God causes all things - the Bible says, God causes all things to work together for good for those who love Him. Religion has given God the credit for the devastation's and the destruction's of life on this earth, but they are not of God. They are not of God!!!

We don't need to beg Jesus for help in the things we face, we can thank Him for what He's done in them, for they aren't unknown to Him: He's been in them, preparing them for us to reap favorable results. If we can look beyond the furnishings of the misery or devastation or shock that we are facing, and see instead the less visible truth of Jesus' prior preparedness of it all for our victory, then we'll access that victory. He has 'been there and done that', and brought it all to a successful conclusion. The manifestation of the victory in our physical world requires our belief.

Let's continue from where the last chapter ended, with Ecclesiastes 3:15:

> *"That which is has already been, And what is to be has already been;"*

'That which is has already been'. In other words, God has seen the thing that's challenging you, before it arrived. It's not new to Him, He visited it to prepare it for your arrival. He continues, 'And what is to be has already been.' That covers the whole gamut of everything that we are or ever will face. Our future is already a past-tense experience for God, though we might wish it was that way for us as well!

The above scripture is written in the eternal-realm language we discussed in the previous chapter: language from outside of time and distance. What is to be has already been. That's like Revelation 13:8, where it says Jesus **is** the Lamb slain from the foundation of the world, rather than 'He was God's plan from the foundation of the world.'

Jesus only showed up historically two thousand years ago. It's hard to comprehend words that speak to us from the heavens, from eternity. Jesus used this eternal perspective in the oft-quoted John 16:33:

> *"These things I have spoken to you, that in Me you may have peace. In the world you will have tribulation; but be of good cheer, I have overcome the world."*

In the future we 'will have' (future tense) tribulation. But Ecclesiastes 3 says that what will be has already been! Jesus goes on to say, "But I have overcome the world" - past tense. From a natural time perspective, Jesus was speaking from before the Cross, but the tenses He used were as if its victory had already been achieved. He's saying, "You will have...but I already have." He has overcome the tribulations of our future experiences in the world.

Go with me to 2 Timothy 1:9-10:

> *2Ti 1:9-10 "who has saved us and called us with a holy calling, not according to our works, but according to His own purpose and grace which was given to us in Christ Jesus before time began, but has now been revealed by the appearing of our Savior Jesus Christ, who has abolished death and brought life and immortality to light through the gospel,"*

If we consolidate those two verses, we read: "He has saved us and called us according to His own purpose and grace, which was given to us in Christ **before** time began, but has now been revealed by Jesus' appearing." We are again seeing the language that speaks from the timeless realm of eternity, outside the limitations of time and distance. And it's speaking to us in the 'now' of Jesus' appearing. Our minds haven't been trained to comprehend these concepts. Paul is saying that, in time, God demonstrated the Lamb slain from the foundation of the world. Personally, I struggle to wrap my mind around that; it must be one of the reasons why Hebrews 11:3 says, "By faith we understand..."

I've discovered that if we can agree that the bible is true, and therefore, that if it says something, we can believe it, and so by faith we can accept it - then we'll find our minds receiving more and more understanding. We begin to work between the two, as the heroes of faith did, seeing the promises from afar although they didn't receive them. They saw them out in the eternal realm, were persuaded of them, embraced them, and began to change their confession. They had a visual acuity that transcended the natural realm of time and distance, that allowed them to hear the voice of God and understand that there was a future and a past, but it was all "now" with God.

Understanding will come to us, for we have the Holy Spirit dwelling in us as Teacher and Revelator - a privilege the ancient heroes did not share.

We were in 1 Peter 3:18, near the beginning of this teaching, lets head back there:

> *1Pe 3:18-20 "For Christ also suffered once for sins, the just for the unjust, that He might bring us to God, being put to death in the flesh but made alive by the Spirit, by whom also He went and preached to the spirits in prison, who formerly were disobedient, when once the Divine longsuffering waited in the days of Noah, while the ark was being prepared,"*

When Peter says in verse 18 that Jesus was put to death in the flesh but made alive by the Spirit, there is more there than jumps out at a casual reading. He is telling us that once Jesus died and was no longer limited by the constraints of a physical body, the eternal realm became His performance arena. Two timeless, everlasting-to-

54

everlasting 'days' are somewhat different from two earthly days! Once in that realm He moved into the section that constitutes our historical time and went to work. This is backed up by verse 18, where it says He suffered for our sins 'so that He might bring us to God.' It was then that He brought you and me, and everyone who has ever lived, past, present or future, to God. He took us into the future, time-wise, but also went back in time to Noah's day.

Hebrews 4:14 has something to add:

> *Heb 4:14 "Seeing then that we have a great High Priest who has passed through the heavens, Jesus the Son of God, let us hold fast our confession."*

We saw in the previous chapter that the heavens aren't controlled by time or distance, so they are the eternal realm. At first glance, it looks as if Jesus, our great High Priest, passed through the heavens on His way to the Father. But the Greek word translated as 'passed through,' *dierchomai*, apart from the sense of traversing, also includes the meanings 'to come and go, go about, go everywhere, travel over, throughout, abroad.'

The sense is not of a direct arrow-flight from the tomb through the heavens. During what we label a three-day time period, Jesus was traversing the realm of eternity, "coming and going everywhere and all throughout", accomplishing everything that was necessary for the redemption, safety and security of mankind from beginning to end of history.

These verses tell us that this is a finished work. There are no unvisited locations, conditions, opportunities or spots. No one can ever say to me, "Mike, I'm in a really tight spot," without me being able to respond in truth,

"Maybe so, but Jesus has already been there, so there is a way through and in this situation."

Jesus didn't go to take a look at what we'll face in life, or to make notes. He went to tenderize and precondition it so that when we arrive there each of us can make the best of it rather than succumb to the worst. Life has extreme moments, many of them, for all of us, as Jesus acknowledged when He said, "In the world you will have tribulation". Let's not forget that He added, "but be of good cheer, I have overcome the world" - and that's exactly the point!

The moments of this world, the spots and situations, want us to go down and under. We may now know Jesus has been there and defeated them, providing a favorable outcome for us, and that there are no unvisited occasions or opportunities, but - and this is vitally important - there *is* untapped knowledge and expectation.

The bible says that God's people are destroyed by lack of knowledge. Jesus wants us to be aware of what He has done for us, and Satan and religion are desperate to limit that knowledge. An example from my life is the scripture that forms the premise of this book, John 14:1-3. As a young believer, all I saw in it was that when I die, Jesus has prepared a place for me. I hung onto that through my time in Vietnam. Others, who knew God had also prepared something for here and now, wrote Psalm 91 across their helmets. Back then I didn't have that understanding. It narrowed my focus, but it still got me through!

Lack of knowledge places us in a position of weakness when we come up against 'a moment.' Meanwhile, the reality is that it is full of Jesus' preparation and He is waiting for us to expect and tap into His victory. No matter what the prognosis is, regardless of the situation, we can have peace and an untroubled heart. These are not light words. They apply to any and every life situation into which we are hurled. Because of Jesus' preparation and victory, we can meet the situation with our heads up and say,

"I know that you paint a rather tragic picture. I know that you present an arrogant front that would suggest my destruction. However, I want *you* to know that *I* know that Jesus visited you from generations and centuries past, and He has prepared you to render favorable regard to me!!"

Psalm 91 says,

> *Ps 91:7 "A thousand may fall at your side, and ten thousand at your right hand; But it shall not come near you."*

That means it doesn't make any difference what the prognosis is, or that nobody survives this kind of cancer or HIV or whatever it is. We are enabled by what Jesus has done, to encounter the situation and acknowledge its preparedness to be transformed in our favor.

Intrinsic to the next example of time is again the sense of Jesus going ahead, then coming back to gather us, and then accompanying us into the future and all it holds. The scripture is John 13:36, where Peter hears that Jesus is leaving, and Peter wants to know if he can go with Him:

> *Joh 13:36 Simon Peter said to Him, "Lord, where are You going?" Jesus answered him, "Where I am going you cannot follow Me now, but you shall follow Me afterward."*

This has generally been interpreted as referring exclusively to Jesus' upcoming crucifixion and Peter's subsequent execution by the same means, but there is more to be found if we dig a little.

'Follow', *akoloutheo*, is formed from a particle of union and the idea of a road. It means, 'to be in the same way with someone, or to accompany.' The sense is therefore of traveling together, as when Peter, Andrew, James and John left their nets and joined Jesus, and this is increased by the continuation of the conversation in the first verses of what we call Chapter 14. Peter could not at that moment in physical time accompany Jesus, to the Cross or in life, but the intent in Jesus' words, above, is that things will change, He will come back to get His friend and walk with him through all the moments of his life and eventual death.

Earlier in this book we saw that the literal interpretation of John 14:2, "I go to prepare a place for you," is, "I go to prepare a place *with* you." That's consistent with being 'crucified with Christ, buried with Christ, raised with Christ and seated with Christ.' Way back then Jesus took us with Him to visit all the spots and conditions of our lives so that they now recognize us and acknowledge our victory over them, through Him, when we get there.

2 Corinthians 5:14 tells us that if One died for all, then all died. In the next verse, it says that we should therefore no longer live for ourselves but for Christ who died for us and rose again. 'For,' *huper*, also means, 'as us' or 'regarding/seeing us'. Christ died as us and seeing us, and we should no longer live as ourselves but as Him, seeing Him who saw us. Again it's the language of another realm, to which our brains must learn to adapt.

Jesus traversed eternity with us, affecting our historical lives if we can believe and consequently utilize that fact. But eternity is forever now, and as He promised repeatedly, He will always be present - or rather, He *is* always present! He said, "Lo, I am with you always," as well as, "I will return repeatedly to associate you with Me, identifying you with Me, that where I am you may be also."

Although we live in an eternal 'now' moment, we also have a future, places where we are yet to be. There is a distorted teaching doing the rounds about the sovereignty of God, which implies that God has all things under control (which means He gives permission for all the bad 'stuff'). I beg to differ. God said, "Let Us make mankind in Our image, according to Our likeness, and let **them** have dominion." Scripture bears that out from beginning to end.

People shake their heads and say in stern tones, "You just don't know where you'll be tomorrow or what tomorrow will bring." We might not know the specifics but we can certainly have an expectation of good surprises, according to God-breathed promises like Jeremiah 29:11: "I know the plans I have for you, plans for welfare and not calamity, to give you a future and an expected end." Or Psalm 91:16, "With long life I will satisfy you and let you see My salvation."

Let's dig around this subject some more. What are we supposed to think about the future? We can agree that Jesus has already been there, and been there with us in Him. We can agree that even now He *is* there, since He's omnipresent in eternity as well as everywhere else. Now, can it be possible, can we say that we are even now with Him somewhere in our future??

There's a passage in Genesis that plays with this thought:

> *Gen 17:4 "As for Me, behold, My covenant is with you, and you shall be a father of many nations. No longer shall your name be called Abram, but your name shall be Abraham; for I have made you a father of many nations.*

Here we have it again: "You *shall be*, for I *have made* you."

God didn't say, "You shall be for I have prepared something for you." It was already done. We can plug a few other things in there too: "You shall be whole for I have made you whole." "You shall be prosperous for I have made you prosperous." "You shall be healed for I have made you healed."

Here's a paraphrase of God's words to Abraham: "You shall be the father of many nations, because *I have made* (past tense) you the father; for *what will be has already been.*" God is speaking to him from the perspective of Abraham being somewhere in his own future - looking very paternal and not at all childless. Abraham is somewhere in his future, looking much better than he does in the historical present.

In the light of this, how do we react to a negative diagnosis (assuming that the diagnosis is correct and based on fact)? What do we do with it? There will be as many factual diagnoses, marital, relational, physical, as there are readers of this book. Do we 'follow' them, i.e. join ourselves to them accompany them as the disciples accompanied Jesus?

What did Jesus say?

"Follow Me."

How do we 'follow' Him when our business has been diagnosed with terminal bankruptcy?

Firstly, we need to differentiate between a diagnosis and a prognosis. A diagnosis is a statement of existing facts. A prognosis is man's evaluation of what those facts portend for the future. We can choose whether to join ourselves to man's prognosis, or see Jesus and His preparation of this moment on the other side of it.

If someone asked my opinion about their diagnosis of bankruptcy, I'd say, "That's the fact. It's standing alone at a crossroads from which two roads diverge. You can travel along one road together with the seemingly inevitable prognosis of the loss of your business and possessions, and buddy up with it, get in union with, accompany it, and ignore Jesus' preconditioning of it. Or you can take the other road, yoking yourself up with Jesus' previous visit to the situation with you, and His victory on your behalf over it. On that road you can see yourself with Him in your future, looking much better than you do at the moment."

I was faced with those choices many years ago when I suffered from extreme depression. I didn't have the revelation of this teaching yet, but as my wife and I held onto the Word, I was slowly healed. Some days were better, some were back in the pit, but those huge tsunamis of depression arrived at longer and longer intervals. I didn't realize that Jesus was on the other side of the tidal wave with me. Now, from the other side, I look a whole lot better than I did back then!

There's something more I'd like you to see in John.

61

John 12:26 "If anyone serves Me, let him follow Me; and where I am, there My servant will be also. If anyone serves Me, him My Father will honor."

There's that word 'follow' again, so the sentence could read, 'If anyone serves Me, let him be in union with Me, accompany Me and join himself to Me.' Serving Jesus means being honored by Father God. Jesus once said that He did not come to be served but to serve. In the verse above, serving Him means honoring Him by coming into union with Him, and that includes all that He has done for us.

Jesus endured the Cross, died and rose again, not only to open the way for our eternal salvation, but also so that our life could be experientially blessed, so that the favorable regard of our grace-filled God could rest upon us at every moment and in every situation and circumstance, and so that we could know the marvelous, great love with which He loves us, and the exceeding kindness of His riches in grace toward us at all times.

The verse quoted above also makes it clear that if we unite ourselves with Jesus, then wherever He is, there we will be too. "Accompany Me, and where I am, there my servant (us) will be." The words ring with an echo of, "You shall be, for I have made..."

Let me conclude returning to Ecclesiastes 3.

Ecc 3:12 " I know that nothing is better for them than to rejoice, and to do good in their lives,"

The word 'and' is not there in the literal translation. The verse should read, "I know there is nothing better for them to do than to rejoice to do good in their lives," or could be equally correctly rendered as: "to rejoice to bring to pass [good, bounty, prosperity, favor] in their lives." Rejoicing in the preparation Jesus has done/brought to pass in all our spots and situations releases the [good, prosperity, bounty, favor] into our life!

Rejoicing is a beautiful way of acknowledging that we know that the spots have been prepared by Jesus for our arrival. Threatening situations have a habit of ambushing us. We're suddenly engulfed in a cell of deep darkness where we crash into imaginary obstacles in our panicky efforts to escape. If we can find the trust and belief to begin praising God for His pre-preparedness of the circumstance, it's as if concealed lighting begins to glow and shortly there's enough illumination to recognize the room and see the way through or out that Jesus provided.

Rejoice, be thankful, praise - any action that expresses belief in the finished work that Jesus has done in advance of our arrival. Rejoice and be glad in the fact that these circumstances have already been prepared to surrender good to us, to bow down before us because we are in Jesus and He identifies us with Him and as Him.

Conclusion

It is my hope and prayer that all who have read this book will close it with a deeper understanding of the completed work Jesus accomplished on the Cross, and of how it applies to all the moments, spots, conditions, locations and situations we face **now** - not only at some intangible future time but now. We can experience peace and a confident sense of victory in the midst of life's storms when we know in that deep place in our heart, that our God has Been There and Done 'That' - everything necessary for victory - in our specific tribulation. He traversed eternity with us and for us, long ago in the future! Believing it is the key that unlocks everything that magnificent Love suffered so much and so powerfully for, on our behalf.

www.ingramcontent.com/pod-product-compliance
Lightning Source LLC
Chambersburg PA
CBHW060039050426
42448CB00012B/3074